Responding to the calling of God in our life requires several things. These include a desire to listen for His calling, a recognition of that calling when we hear it, and a willingness to follow in obedience. It seems we often miss the sacred calling of God in our life because we are looking for some grand and noble task while God is calling us to a life set apart for Him even, and perhaps especially, in the midst of everyday tasks.

This book is dedicated in grateful acknowledgment to God who continues to give me an understanding of His calling in my life. I thank the encouragers in my life who help me stay focused on the things God has called me to do. And I thank the Deer Run congregation and my family — each of them helps me in a great way to live out the calling and gifting God has put in my life. To all of these, and to you my readers, thank you!

Table of Contents

Here Am I, . . .

Introduction

Calling. Sacred Calling. Is there a difference? How can God's Word help us to view our calling in life as a sacred calling no matter what career path we feel called into? This devotional journal is designed to help you spend time with God to understand how He has created people, including you, to be set apart for His exclusive use no matter what our skills, interests, or careers happen to be. Turn your calling into a sacred calling simply by saying to God, "Here Am I."

You may use this book as a thirty-one day devotional or go through it at whatever pace suits you. Take your time to let each statement about God's calling sink deeply into your being. The book is designed to be used as both a devotional and a journal as you discover what God says about you.

Each topic follows the same three-page format. The first page is simply a statement of that day's focus and a scripture reference to get you started in God's Word. Look up the scripture reference and meditate on God's Word about the calling He desires for you to respond to.

The second page is some devotional writing that has come from my prayer time focused on that day's subject. It will include questions to help you think more clearly about the sacred calling in your life. There will also be some devotional thoughts to help you as you seek to understand how to apply God's calling to your everyday life. As you go through this page of each day's topic, spend time with God learning how to have a greater grasp of His sacred calling in your life.

The third page is your turn to make this devotional even more personal! It contains a heading of the day's topic, some prayer points to help direct your prayers for yourself and others, and then a blank lined page. This is for you to record your interaction with God each day. Jot down your thoughts, your prayers, other scriptures that God brings to mind during your time with Him, and/or changes in your attitude or actions that He reveals you need to make. Use this journal page to help you remember and to help you grow.

In prayer,
Tom Lemler
Impact Prayer Ministry

Day One

Called

To Belong

(Romans 1:6)

Called To Belong

Where do you belong? Who do you belong to? Which of those questions are you most comfortable with? Why? Have others ever made you believe you didn't belong in a particular group or situation that you wanted to be a part of? In what way? How did you feel? What does it take to make you feel you fit in or belong in a place or situation? Is an invitation enough? Why? How involved are you in helping others feel they belong in groups you are a part of? How has God backed up His invitation of belonging with substance that makes you know you belong?

Most of us have a desire to feel useful and needed — to know we belong wherever we are. We've also accepted invitations to places where we've felt out of place as the invitation alone was not enough to give us a sense of belonging. When God calls us to belong, it is not an invitation to join a group or club; rather it is calling us to belong to Jesus. It is Christ who gives us a place to belong when He is the One we belong to. Belonging to Christ means we belong wherever He is and wherever He sends us. It also means others who belong to Christ deserve our acceptance as well.

9

Called To Belong

As you pray about where you belong, begin with a recognition of who you belong to. Pray that you would grow in your understanding of what it means each day to belong to Christ. Pray that you would have the courage to accept God's calling in your life — both in belonging to Him and in belonging wherever He has work for you to do. Pray about how you make others feel when they are around you. Pray for a sense of community and belonging with all who are in Christ.

Day Two

Called

To Be a Blessing

(1 Peter 3:9)

Called To Be a Blessing

Who has been the greatest blessing to you recently? Why? Would your name be someone else's answer to that question? Why? What does a blessing look like to you? Is that answer different depending on if you are giving or receiving the blessing? Why? Have you ever been intentional about being a blessing to someone? Did it work? How did that effort affect you? Why? Is there someone that comes to mind right now that you could be a blessing to? What will you do about it?

As a Christian, it shouldn't take long to think of someone that has been a blessing to you — even if (and that's a big if) the only one on that list is Jesus himself. I think the bigger question for us to wrestle with, is who am I being a blessing to. The way we live life, the way we speak, the way we listen, the way we give, even the way we receive are all ways that our life can be a blessing to someone else. While blessing those who bless us should be an easy thing to do, God calls us to also be a blessing to those who do not treat us, or Him, as they should. In blessing others, we find God's blessing grows in our life.

Called To Be a Blessing

As you pray about the blessings you receive, ask God to help you be a blessing to the people around you. Pray for the wisdom to know how to be a blessing to people regardless of how they treat you. Pray that you would know the greater blessing which comes from giving of yourself to help others. Pray that your response to God would assure you of an inherited blessing as you treat others as He would have you do. Pray that you would be mindful of the opportunities God gives you to bless others.

_____

_____

_____

_____

_____

_____

_____

_____

_____

_____

_____

_____

Day Three

Called

To Be a

Child of God

(1 John 3:1)

Called To Be a Child of God

Who are your parents? What influence have they had on the way you live? Why? What were some expectations of you as a child in your family? Were there responsibilities and privileges as well? In what way? If you have children, what do you expect from them? What benefits do they have as your child? What do you think of when you hear the word child? Does that answer influence how you feel about being called a child? In what way? How does God's love influence your desire to be called His child?

There is little that makes me more proud than to have my parents refer to me as their son when they are talking to others. It is meaningful because I know the love and pride they convey with that word. When John describes the depth of God's love, he does so by indicating a Father who lavishes His love upon me to the extent of calling me His child. While the honor of being called a child of God is great, so are the responsibilities and privileges that come with that position. As a child of God I not only inherit that which belongs to the Father, but I also reflect Him to the people that know me as His child.

15

Called To Be a Child of God

As you pray about being called a child of God, ask God to help you know the love He pours out upon you. Pray that you would make the most of the honor and privilege that comes from being a child of God. Pray that you would live up to the expectations that God has for you. Pray for God's help in living a life that honors your Father well and reflects Him to the people around you. Pray that you would always find joy in being known as a child of God.

_____

_____

_____

_____

_____

_____

_____

_____

_____

_____

_____

_____

_____

Day Four

Called

To Be Chosen

(Revelation 17:14)

Called To Be Chosen

Have you ever been a part of the choosing of teams? How did you feel while waiting to be chosen? Why? Were you ever the one to do the choosing? How did that feel? Why? How does the perceived importance of the one doing the choosing influence your feelings about being chosen? What if the one choosing is God? Have you ever been chosen for something that you really wanted but knew you weren't fully qualified for? What did being chosen do for your confidence? How comfortable are you with the idea of being chosen by God? Why?

It seems I have more experience of wanting something and not being chosen than of being chosen, but I suppose that makes being chosen by God even more spectacular for me. To know I will be with Jesus in the midst of His victory is an incredible thing. To be called by the creator of the universe as His chosen one lifts me to a level that is far beyond what being chosen for anything else could do. The good news that Jesus wants us to share is that He has called everyone who will respond to be His chosen and faithful followers. We are chosen not because of us, but because of Him.

Called To Be Chosen

As you pray about being called by God, ask Him to make you more aware of how valuable you are to Him.   Pray that you would live life with the knowledge that God has chosen you to be His. Pray for a life of faithfulness that not only accepts being chosen by God, but shares that relationship with others.   Pray that you would see value in each person you meet, knowing that God chooses all who would come to Him.   Pray for the courage to live as one chosen by God.

_____

_____

_____

_____

_____

_____

_____

_____

_____

_____

_____

_____

Day Five

Called

To Be

Counted Worthy

(2 Thessalonians 1:11)

Called To Be Counted Worthy

Are there people in your life who see you as being worth more than you see yourself? What do you think they see that you can't? Why? Do you have a tendency to over value yourself or under value yourself? What would those closest to you say? Why? What influence does being valued by others have on your feelings of worthiness? Does being considered worthy increase your desire to live up to the worthiness others see in you? How will being counted worthy by God help you to live and work more fully in His power?

When we compare ourselves to the holiness of Jesus, it should quickly become apparent that we will never be worthy on our own. The good news is that Jesus sees beyond our choices, both good and bad, and sees the individual that has been created in His image. He chooses to count us worthy because of His great love for us. Even in the midst of our sin, God counted us worthy of His love displayed in the death, burial, and resurrection of Jesus. Being counted worthy by God, even when we know we're not, ought to compel us to see others from the same perspective with which God views us.

21

Called To Be Counted Worthy

As you pray about being counted worthy by God, ask God to encourage you through His desire for you to be His. Pray that you would look beyond your limitations and faults to see all that God can do in and through you because He counts you worthy. Pray for a heart of compassion for those who have been knocked down by this world and need to know that God has called them to be counted worthy. Pray for the humility needed to see others as God sees them.

_____

_____

_____

_____

_____

_____

_____

_____

_____

_____

_____

_____

_____

Day Six

Called

To Eternal Glory

(1 Peter 5:10)

Called To Eternal Glory

What is the most glorious thing you have ever seen? How long did that glory last? Why? What is it that gives something its glory? What things cause that glory to fade? How does a focus on the difficulties of life affect your view of the future? Why? What would a continual focus on a future of eternal glory do to your view of the suffering you experience? Why? Which is easier to focus on, the present or the future? Which has the greater reward? What will you do to live as one who has been called to an eternal glory?

Many people try to overcome discouragement by seeking out something new and shiny to lift their mood. Whatever we purchase to get us through our struggles here on earth will eventually wear out and lose its glory and our encouragement is short-lived. When God calls us to an eternal glory, He gives us glimpses of it throughout life. In this way, the glory which carries us through our suffering doesn't fade; rather it is ever-increasing until we experience it in its fullness with Christ. While our enemy wants us to focus on the troubles of life so that we would give up, God calls us to focus on an eternal glory for all who are faithful.

Called To Eternal Glory

As you pray about being called to an eternal glory, ask God to help you keep your eyes fixed on the glory that is found in Him. Pray that you would not lose heart in the midst of life's hardships. Pray that your life and words would be reminders to others of the glory that is yet to come. Pray that you would know the greatness of God's glory as you allow it to give perspective to your current sufferings. Pray for the courage to allow God to strengthen you as you rest in Him.

_____

_____

_____

_____

_____

_____

_____

_____

_____

_____

_____

_____

Day Seven

Called

To Be Faithful

(Revelation 14:12)

Called To Be Faithful

How often do you feel like giving up? Why? Do you? Are there things you ought to give up on? What things should you never give up on? How do you know the difference? When you think of being faithful, is there a specific person that comes to mind? Who? Why? Do you think of yourself as a faithful person? Why? Would the people who know you best agree? Why? How should being called by God to be faithful influence the way you view your ability to be faithful and the patience you approach life with?

When I think about being faithful, I think more about a steadfast pursuit of something than I think about having actually arrived. The destination is great, but many times our impatience causes us to change course before we accomplish what God desires to do in and through us. God's desire is that weariness or distraction would not cause us to give up before we reap the harvest of righteousness He has in store for us. When we respond to God's call to be faithful with a steadfast "Here am I", we commit to a life that doesn't give up in our pursuit of Him. In a world filled with broken promises, be one who is faithful.

27

Called To Be Faithful

As you pray about being faithful, ask God to help you see your decisions and actions from an eternal perspective. Pray that you would not become weary in doing good. Pray that the evil in the world would not distract you nor entice you into a life that is unfaithful. Pray for the wisdom to understand the direction God has set forth in His Word, and for the courage to be steadfast in following His direction no matter what. Pray that your life would be an example to others.

_____

_____

_____

_____

_____

_____

_____

_____

_____

_____

_____

_____

_____

Day Eight

Called

To Fellowship

(1 Corinthians 1:9)

Called To Fellowship

Who are the people you like being with the most? Why? Do you consider yourself a "people person" or not? How does that influence your desire to be with people? How much time do you spend with God? What does that time look like? How do you feel about God calling you into fellowship with Jesus? Does knowing He desires fellowship with you determine how much time you spend with Him? Why? Does that fellowship make a difference in the fellowship you have with others? In what way?

While it can be somewhat confusing to figure out if we belong in the fellowship of a group of people, God leaves no doubt about His desire when He calls us into fellowship with His Son. It is in the context of this fellowship that He also calls us into fellowship with one another. Through our fellowship with God we ought to find commonality to have fellowship with others. When I think of fellowship with God, I consider one of my favorite Bible characters — Enoch, a man who walked with God in such a way that one day his daily walk continued uninterrupted from this earth to God's presence.

Called To Fellowship

As you pray, ask God to help you fully believe His invitation to a greater fellowship with Jesus. Pray that being called into fellowship would increase your desire and commitment to spend time with God. Pray that you would be known as one who walks with God. Pray that your fellowship with other believers would grow as you deepen your fellowship with God. Pray that you would be actively involved in making others aware of God's desire to have fellowship with them.

_____

_____

_____

_____

_____

_____

_____

_____

_____

_____

_____

_____

_____

Day Nine

Called

For God's Purpose

(Romans 8:28)

Called For God's Purpose

Does what you do each day have a purpose? What is it? Does knowing the answer to that help to motivate you to do what only you can do? Why? What if you don't know the purpose? Does not knowing mean there isn't a purpose? Explain. What are some of God's purposes for His children that He has revealed in His Word? Will pursuing those purposes give you greater belief in the purpose He has for you? Why? How will living as one called according to God's purpose change the way you view tasks and circumstances that you don't understand?

Often just knowing there is purpose to our work makes it more enjoyable, even if we don't fully understand the purpose. The Bible gives us many purposes for the believer's life which generally revolve around making Christ known and glorifying our Father. When we live with a pursuit of the holy purposes of God, we learn to trust that he can use our ordinary tasks of life to accomplish His extraordinary purpose. As God calls you for His purpose, trust Him to do good works through you and to work all of your circumstances together for good.

33

Called For God's Purpose

As you pray, ask God to increase your faith so that you would have a greater trust in the goodness of His purposes. Pray that you would respond in a positive way to God's desire that your life fulfill the purposes He has revealed in scripture. Pray that God would open your eyes to see how He has worked, and continues to work, in the details of your life in order to accomplish His good purpose. Pray that you would be patient in waiting for God's purpose to be completed in His time.

_____

_____

_____

_____

_____

_____

_____

_____

_____

_____

_____

_____

Day Ten

Called

To Be Free

(Galatians 5:13)

Called To Be Free

Do you ever feel stuck, or trapped, in some situation of life? Why? How much effort do you put into getting out of those situations? Why? Do you think freedom is more about what you can do or about what you don't have to do? What's the difference? Are there things you enjoy doing because you have the freedom to do them that you would not enjoy if it was something you had to do? Why? What is God's idea of freedom when He calls you to be free? Explain. How does God want you to use the freedom He has called you to?

Freedom is one of those words that get thrown around a lot with most people having their own idea of what it means based on what they want to be free from or what they want to be free to do. God's desire is that we would find freedom in Christ that sets us completely free from the bondage of sin. But not only does He want us to be free from the burdens produced by sin, He wants us to be free to do the works produced by love. Being set free leaves us with a choice on how we use that freedom and God calls us to live life free to love as He loves and to serve with complete humility just as He has served us.

Called To Be Free

As you pray, ask God to make known to you the glorious riches of the freedom you have in Christ. Pray that you would understand both what you have been set free from and what you have been set free for. Pray about how God would have you use the freedom He has given. Pray for the courage to live as one who is free to love and serve others. Pray that your life would be an example to others who need to know how to live a life of freedom.

_____

_____

_____

_____

_____

_____

_____

_____

_____

_____

_____

_____

_____

Day Eleven

Called

To Be a

Friend of God

(John 15:15)

Called To Be a Friend of God

Who are your friends? Who considers you to be their friend? Why? What do you look for in a friend? Why? Have you ever tried to have a friendship with someone that didn't seem to want to be friends? Did it work? Why? What would you do for your true friends? What would they do for you? Why? Have you ever had a relationship that began as something other than friends but grew into a friendship? What changed? What does it mean to you to be called a friend of God? What will you do with that friendship?

It is difficult to maintain a friendship for very long if it appears to be one-sided with little to no effort being put forth by the other person. As Christians, we are not only called to be a friend of God, He calls us His friend. Not only should our friendship with God lead us to share with Him in every aspect of our life, His friendship with us results in Him making Himself known to us through His Word and His Spirit. As a friend, He holds nothing back that would be a benefit to us. As God, He knows perfectly the things that are for our good and the things which would bring harm. As both, He knows and loves us as no one else can.

Called To Be a Friend of God

As you pray, ask God to help you see clearly His desire to have you as a friend. Pray that you would live as a friend of God. Pray that your friendship with God would lead you to be a better friend to others. Pray for wisdom in knowing and understanding the things of God. Pray for courage in upholding your side of a friendship with God. Pray about how you will share your friendship with the hurting and lonely around you who need to know God's love.

_____

_____

_____

_____

_____

_____

_____

_____

_____

_____

_____

_____

_____

Day Twelve

Called

To Be Genuine

(1 Corinthians 1:26)

Called To Be Genuine

How many people know the real you? Are you sure? How do you feel when someone presents themselves to others as something they are not? Why? Are there things about your past, or present, that you try to keep secret? Why? How have those things been a part of you becoming who you are today? How does remembering where you've come from help you see how God has worked in your life? Who has been an example to you as one who is genuine? In what way? Who needs to see the real you?

Regardless of our background, there are usually things from our past that we would just as soon pretend never happened. Growth is intended to bring us to a place that is often different from where we began. For many who have reached the place of life they desire, there is a great temptation to act as if we've always been where we are. When done with wisdom and discretion, being genuine about who we were before Christ gives us great opportunity to share about the transformation He has done in our life. Our struggles not only help us to grow, when we are genuine they become examples for others.

Called To Be Genuine

As you pray about being genuine, ask God to help you remember the what and where of who you were before you responded to His call. Pray that you would allow God to use the real you to show His power to the people around you. Pray that God would reveal, and deal with, any areas of pretense that you have harbored in your life. Pray for the discretion needed for you to be genuine in ways that are helpful to others. Pray with thanksgiving for a God who is genuine.

_____

_____

_____

_____

_____

_____

_____

_____

_____

_____

_____

_____

Day Thirteen

Called

To a Glorious

Inheritance

(Ephesians 1:18)

Called To a Glorious Inheritance

Have you ever inherited something? Was it something you were impressed with, or not? Why? What would you do if you were to inherit a fortune or substantial piece of property? Would it be possible to keep it a secret? Why? What is the longest you have had to wait for something that you were expecting and looking forward to? Was the wait worth it? Why? How does hope keep you looking forward to what is still ahead? How does this calling of God strengthen the hope you live with each day?

Many people are fascinated with stories of ordinary people who are left a fortune by a relative they didn't even know they had. I suppose such stories give hope that perhaps they too could inherit such a windfall. Yet none of these stories will ever measure up to the glorious inheritance each of us is called to as a child of God. This inheritance doesn't come from an unknown relative and it isn't the result of chance. It is a promise from God to both those who are near and those who are far off, that all would draw near can look forward with a confident hope that they too can share in His inheritance.

Called To a Glorious Inheritance

As you pray about the inheritance you are called to, ask God to fill you with the hope of glory. Pray that you would find comfort in the day to day struggles of life as you live with confidence in the glorious inheritance to which you are called. Pray for a greater awareness of God's love as you share with others about how they too have been called to share in this inheritance from God. Pray that God would help you to hold fast to the hope you have in Jesus as you look forward to His return.

_____

_____

_____

_____

_____

_____

_____

_____

_____

_____

_____

_____

_____

Day Fourteen

Called

To Hear

(Luke 8:8)

Called To Hear

Is it possible to listen to someone without hearing what they are really saying? What does it take for you to hear what people are actually saying? Does listening beyond the surface of a conversation come easy to you? How good are you at listening to God? Do you think He would say that you are one who "has ears to hear"? Why? Should hearing what God has said in His Word change the way you do life? In what way? Does it? How does a practice of listening to God change the way that you hear what others are saying?

It has been said that the average person listens more for the purpose of responding rather than understanding. It seems that even in the days of Jesus, the crowds would gather and listen to His words with little attempt to understand what He was saying, let alone put His words into practice. As Christians, God calls us to use what He has given us in order to actually hear what He has to say. Those who "have ears to hear" should make it a practice to not only hear what God has said, but to incorporate His words into how we live life. As God calls each of us to hear what He says, His desire is that we would do what He says.

48

Called To Hear

As you pray about how you listen to God, ask Him to open your ears to the truth of His Word. Pray that you would be one who desires to hear from God as you spend time with Him in prayer and His Word. Pray that you would grow in the way that you listen so that you would also hear beyond the surface in what others say to you. Pray that you would learn to seek understanding of what you hear before responding. Pray that your life would reflect an active hearing of God's Word.

_____

_____

_____

_____

_____

_____

_____

_____

_____

_____

_____

_____

_____

Day Fifteen

Called

To Holiness

(1 Corinthians 1:2)

Called To Holiness

Do you have things that are only used for special purposes? Why? Do those things ever become unsuitable for their intended purposes? Explain. What comes to your mind when someone talks about living a life of holiness? Do you think it is possible? Why? Where does holiness begin? When something, or someone, is holy, what does it take to keep it that way? Explain. How important is holiness to God? What will it take for holiness to be just as important to you as it is to God?

Whether it is the good china, special attire, or holiday decorations, most of us have things that we treat as special — things set apart for a specific use or purpose. Being called to holiness means that we are that special thing to God. Not that we've been put on a shelf for some future time, but that we've been called by God for His special use and purpose. A life of holiness requires that we take every thought captive as we make choices that lead us to honor God's will and purpose in our life. Responding to God's call to holiness sets us on a path that leads us toward greater obedience to God as we learn to be holy.

51

Called To Holiness

As you pray about being called to holiness, ask God to fill you with the desire to be used by Him. Pray that you would open your mind and spirit to understanding how special you are to God. Pray for the courage to evaluate all of your thoughts and actions to see how well aligned they are with the things of God. Pray for the humility to lead a life set apart for God's exclusive use in such a way that He is seen by those around you. Pray that a desire for holiness would lead you to be holy.

_____

_____

_____

_____

_____

_____

_____

_____

_____

_____

_____

_____

Day Sixteen

Called

To Be Holy

(1 Peter 1:15)

Called To Be Holy

How is being holy related to living a life of holiness? What comes to mind when you think of someone being holy? Is holiness something that you consider attainable in your own life? Why? What specific things need to take place in your life for you to be holy? Who can do those things in your life? Is there a part of holiness that is up to you in addition to the work God does in your life? How does a daily reminder that you've been set free from sin help you to pursue holiness? Why is holiness such a necessary and noble pursuit?

Holiness has to do with belonging to God or being set apart for God's exclusive use. It is such a big part of the identity we ought to have in Christ that this journal spends two days focused on this sacred calling of holiness. Our holiness is only possible as we are purified through the blood of Jesus, but that holiness is maintained as we daily surrender to living a life exclusive to God. It is through, and because of, that cleansing by Jesus that He is able to call us to be holy, just as He is holy. When we live as one set apart for God's use, we seek to live in such a way that our life brings honor and glory to Him.

Called To Be Holy

As you pray about God's call for you to be holy, ask Him to give you the wisdom to live a life that reflects His holiness. Pray that you would always choose the things of life that would lead to purity in your thoughts and actions. Pray that God would purify you from all unrighteousness. Pray for a heart that seeks to honor God in all you do. Pray that you would be free to live exclusively for God. Pray that you would learn to be holy, just as Christ is holy.

_____

_____

_____

_____

_____

_____

_____

_____

_____

_____

_____

_____

Day Seventeen

Called

Into Light

(1 Peter 2:9)

Called Into Light

Have you ever used darkness to get by with things that you should not have done? Why? How does light influence your choices? Are there things that you allow to exist in the shadows of your life that you would rather not be brought to light? What are they? What would God want you to do with them? Will you? How does living in the light make you feel? Why? Should being called into the light change the way the people around you see you? The way they see God? In what ways?

Whether you prefer living in the spotlight or are more comfortable in the background of life, God calls you to step out of the darkness of this world and into His glorious light. This calling isn't about you being more visible, but about Him being more visible through you as you proclaim His praises each day. As we journey further into God's light, it is not just the deeds of darkness we leave behind — we also find the things we've kept in the shadows are exposed for what they are. Responding to God's call to walk in His light isn't about guilt or shame over what is exposed, rather it is about finding freedom to live in that light in a way that glorifies God.

Called Into Light

As you pray about being called into the light, ask God to help you see any areas of darkness that keep you from embracing His light fully. Pray that you would allow Him to transform your mind so that even the hints of darkness would have no appeal to you. Pray that you would constantly praise God as you recall both what He has called you out of and what He has called you into. Pray for God's help in not only walking in His light, but in helping others to see His light.

_____

_____

_____

_____

_____

_____

_____

_____

_____

_____

_____

_____

_____

Day Eighteen

Called

To Live In

Hope

(Ephesians 4:4)

Called To Live In Hope

What does hope mean to you? How do you usually use the word? Do you think that is what God means when He calls you to live in hope? Explain. When is hope most needed? Have you ever been discouraged — perhaps even now? How does hope help you to see that your current circumstances are not permanent? Has anyone ever tried to encourage you with a hope that you knew was iffy at best? Did it help? Why? How does living with one hope differ from what the world offers when it comes to hope?

In a world filled with self-help books and podcasts covering just about any situation imaginable, true hope seems to be a rather elusive thing for many who desperately need it. In our efforts to make sense of a messed-up world, there is only one source that offers real hope in the midst of troubling times. When God calls us to live in hope, it is in the context of being united with Him in a way that ought to unite us with one another. The one hope that can carry us through anything is the assured hope that is available through Jesus Christ. When we live in this hope, we live with something the world both wants and needs.

60

Called To Live In Hope

As you pray about being called to live in hope, ask God to help you to see the various things you have tried to put your hope in. Pray that you would set aside the world's view of hope so that you could live in the one hope that God calls you to. Pray for the courage to share true hope with others even when they think they can find a better hope elsewhere. Pray that your hope in Jesus would help you live in greater unity with others.

_____

_____

_____

_____

_____

_____

_____

_____

_____

_____

_____

_____

_____

Day Nineteen

Called

To Be Loved

(Jude 1:1)

Called To Be Loved

How loved do you feel? Why? Do you ever think you are unlovable? Why? What does it take to make you feel loved?   Does that change based on who the love is coming from? Why? Is unconditional love the same as unconditional approval?   Explain.   How does the love you have experienced from people influence your view of God's love? Should it?   How does knowing that God Himself has called you to be loved by Him change the way you experience His love? Will living as one loved by God change you? Why?

Sometimes the person we think most undeserving of being loved is our self. While there may be a lot of factors which lead us to believe that, the truth is that God has called each of us to be loved by Him! Our actions do matter to God but not in the sense that they increase or decrease His love for us. Even the best love that we experience from people pales in comparison to the purity of the love that only God can give. When God says that He so loved the world that He gave, He means that He loves you and I now and He loved us when we were dead in our sins. Living as one loved by God is indeed a sacred calling.

Called To Be Loved

As you pray about being loved, ask God to bring healing to whatever is in your life that tries to convince you that you are unlovable. Pray that you would seek to please God because of His love rather than seeking God's love by pleasing Him. Pray that any doubts you may have about God's love for you would be dispelled as you respond to His call to be loved. Pray for the courage to live as one loved by God as you represent Him to people who need to experience that same love.

_____

_____

_____

_____

_____

_____

_____

_____

_____

_____

_____

_____

_____

Day Twenty

Called

To Love

(John 15:12)

Called To Love

Who do you love? Do they know it? How? How does being loved change the way you love? What does it mean to love someone? Does that look different based on who it is? Explain. Does the love God wants you to have for others always look like what the other person wants it to? Why? Are there people you don't want to love? Why? How does experiencing God's love for you help you to love people that may be difficult to love? What would God want you to do differently today that would be a response to His call to love others?

While this may seem at first to be the same topic as the previous devotion, God's calling to love is the giving aspect compared to the receiving that is done in being loved. Loving people God's way will always look out for their best even when doing so is not appreciated or desired. Godly love is a giving of our self in order to lift someone else up. Not only has God given us this sacred calling to love, but He demonstrated just how to do that through the sending of His Son to express His love for us. Loving the hard to love is possible only when you realize just how much God has loved you.

Called To Love

As you pray about being called to love, ask God to help you notice the things that people actually need. Pray that you would look to God for the strength and courage to love people you don't like. Pray that you would do the hard work of loving those who are difficult to love. Pray that God would remind you of His great love for you even when you were living as His enemy. Pray that your love for people would help others to know a God who loves them fully.

_____

_____

_____

_____

_____

_____

_____

_____

_____

_____

_____

_____

_____

Day Twenty - One

Called

To Peace

(Colossians 3:15)

Called To Peace

How much peace do you feel in your life at the moment? What do you feel are the causes for that level of peace? Why? Does living with peace require the successful resolution of all conflict? Explain. What role does being thankful have in experiencing peace in all circumstances? Are there specific things that seem to repeatedly rob you of peace? Why? How can identifying those things, and how God was with you the last time those things happened, help you to have greater peace when they reoccur?

The cares of this world seem to do a pretty good job at disrupting the peace God wants us to live with. Since there is no magic wand to get rid of those cares, God calls us to a peace that surpasses all understanding. In the midst of conflict and discouraging circumstances, we can find peace in knowing God has been present before, during, and after all of the things that try to steal our peace. His presence will carry us through the conflicts of life with the peace of knowing the troubles are only temporary. When we live out this sacred calling of peace, we find that our relationship with God, and with others, is transformed.

Called To Peace

As you pray about being called to peace, ask God to remind you of His presence during the times He seems most distant. Pray that you would trust in God's promises when the cares of this world try to destroy the peace He has called you to. Pray that you would have courage in facing conflicts which are beyond your control with a peace that can only come from God. Pray about how your faith will allow you to see God at work in the midst of difficult and trying times.

_____

_____

_____

_____

_____

_____

_____

_____

_____

_____

_____

_____

_____

Day Twenty-Two

Called To Be a Peacemaker

(Matthew 5:9)

Called To Be a Peacemaker

Does your presence in a situation tend to increase the peace or the conflict? Why? How does your response to God's call to peace influence your ability to be a peacemaker? Are there people in your life who have been difficult for you to make peace with? Why? Is it always possible to be at peace with everyone? Explain. What does it take for you to be at peace with God? With others? How can you apply those things to being one who helps others to have peace with God, with you, and with one another?

When we live with the peace that only God can give, He expects us to find ways to make peace even with our enemies. While peace is a two-sided proposition and we can't force someone to a position of peace with us, our responsibility is to do our part as far as peace depends upon us. It is often through the process of listening and forgiveness that we find peace with God and one another and we are able to help others know the peace that comes from God. Living as a peacemaker among people becomes a much easier task when we first have peace with God and work at helping people find peace with Him.

Called To Be a Peacemaker

As you pray about being a peacemaker, ask God to help you know exactly what it is that has brought peace into your life. Pray that you would grow in both listening and forgiving as you make peace with the people around you. Pray that you would have the humility necessary to be available as a peacemaker to those who are caught up in the midst of conflict. Pray for the persistence needed to keep at it when the going gets difficult and peace seems elusive.

_____

_____

_____

_____

_____

_____

_____

_____

_____

_____

_____

_____

_____

Day Twenty-Three

Called

To Sacrifice

(Mark 8:34)

Called To Sacrifice

What do you think is the biggest obstacle to a willingness to sacrifice? Why? Are there things in this life you have sacrificed for in order to have (i.e. car, house, vacation, relationship, etc.)? Why did you sacrifice? Was it worth it? Why? What determines your willingness to sacrifice and the extent to which you are willing to sacrifice? How does seeing a greater future value make you feel about giving up something that has a temporary value? Is there anything more valuable to you than an eternity with God?

I've not yet met anyone who has been able to have everything they wanted at no cost to them. Much of our life seems to be spent evaluating our priorities and determining what we're willing to give up in order to have the things we really want. It is in relationship with God that we begin to see the true value of things and discover that giving up temporary treasures for that which is eternal is worth it no matter the cost. Jesus made it clear in His life and teaching that being His disciple came with a huge cost, yet denying self and dying with Christ yields an outcome that far surpasses the sacrifice of everything we have.

Called To Sacrifice

As you pray about being called to sacrifice, ask God to reveal to you anything which you still cling to that has become more important than Him. Pray that you would consider giving up everything you are and everything you have as being a small sacrifice compared to the surpassing riches of His glory. Pray for the courage to not only surrender the entirety of your life to Christ, but in that surrender to allow Him to use everything under your care for His purposes and glory.

_____

_____

_____

_____

_____

_____

_____

_____

_____

_____

_____

_____

_____

Day Twenty-Four

Called

To Be a Saint

(Romans 1:7)

Called To Be a Saint

What do you think of when you hear the word saint? Why? Who do you first think of when you think about a saint? Why? Is it a word you think of often when considering your own life? Why? How much of your life do you allow God to use? Are you sure? Is there a difference between God using a person's actions and God having exclusive use of a person? Explain. How do you feel about being called by God to be a saint? Why? According to God, what makes a person a saint? Explain.

While common use of the word may make sainthood appear unattainable to the average Christian, God's calling is much broader. In fact, He calls every believer to be a saint — a person set apart for God's exclusive use. In this way, being a saint isn't dependent on our goodness or our special deeds but it is completely dependent on a full surrender to the goodness of God and a willingness to do His work. We don't "earn" the title of saint by our good deeds, rather we live life doing the good works God created in advance for us because we have been called by God to be a saint — and that's what His saints do!

Called To Be a Saint

As you pray about being called to be a saint, ask God to help you evaluate why you do the good that you do. Pray that you would be obedient to the things of God because He has called you to be set apart for Him, not in order to earn some special title. Pray that you would carefully consider what things are appropriate for you to do as one fully surrendered to God. Pray that your life would reflect Jesus to others as you give Him authority over everything you do.

_____
_____
_____
_____
_____
_____
_____
_____
_____
_____
_____
_____

Day Twenty-Five

Called

To Serve

(Mark 10:42-44)

Called To Serve

What does it mean to serve someone? In what ways do others serve you? In what ways do you serve others? Which do you prefer? Why? How does attitude influence the quality of serving you, or someone else, might do? Are there times, or people, you are more willing to serve than others? Why? What makes the difference? What limits did God put on who you should serve? What about on how you should serve? Explain. Does knowing God has called you to serve change your attitude about serving? Why?

Most Christians can quote the words of Jesus when He says, "whoever wants to become great must become servant to all." The problem, however, is that quoting it and living it are two very different things. How we treat others from any walk of life says a lot about how much we've allowed Jesus to have control of our life. Serving others isn't just about doing things for them; it begins with our attitude about them. When we allow Jesus to transform our heart, we learn to willingly serve others because we genuinely care about them. In fact, God says that it is in our serving of others that we actually serve Him.

Called To Serve

As you pray about being called to serve, ask God to help you grow in your desire to serve all people. Pray that you would learn to love people just as God loves them so you would want the very best for them. Pray that you would serve with a transformed heart that helps those you serve to see Jesus. Pray that you would look for opportunities to serve even those whose job it is to serve you. Pray that you would find pleasure in serving God through your service to others.

_____

_____

_____

_____

_____

_____

_____

_____

_____

_____

_____

_____

Day Twenty-Six

Called

To Suffer

(1 Peter 2:20-21)

Called To Suffer

How often do you experience difficult times and think that it just shouldn't be this way? Why? Have you ever learned valuable lessons in the midst of suffering? What? Could they have been learned without the suffering? Why? What does suffering as a result of poor choices teach you? Is that different from what you learn as a result of suffering for doing right? Explain. How is Christ represented in your attitude when you suffer because of what someone else has said or done? Who does your response change the most, you or them?

Suffering seems to be an unavoidable part of life and how we handle it can say a lot to a suffering world that needs to know the peace that only Jesus can bring in the midst of their hurt. When we live with the hope that only Jesus can offer, we find the pain of suffering can be a powerful reminder of how valuable we are to Him. It is in suffering for doing right that the world can see proof of what we believe. Whether the pain is physical, emotional, spiritual, or some combination of all three, learning to endure with patience in the midst of suffering is only possible when our eyes are fixed on the hope that lies ahead.

Called To Suffer

As you pray about being called to suffer, ask God to fill you with a greater hope in the things yet to come. Pray that you would make wise choices that would keep you from suffering for doing wrong. Pray that your suffering would make you more aware of the price Jesus paid for the hope that now dwells within you. Pray that others would know more of your love, and of God's love, as you patiently endure suffering that comes from doing life God's way.

_____

_____

_____

_____

_____

_____

_____

_____

_____

_____

_____

_____

Day Twenty-Seven

Called

To Be Sure

(2 Peter 1:10)

Called To Be Sure

Are there things you are certain about? What? Have you ever been sure about something only to find out later you were wrong? Why? How much power does doubt have in your life? Why? What things tend to feed your doubt? Have you ever been sure of something only to have it not come to pass? Why? What does that do to your sense of certainty about other things? How reliable do you believe God to be? Does His faithfulness give you greater confidence in the things He has called you to? Should it?

Living with certainty in a very uncertain world can be a rather elusive thing. Fortunately, the certainty that you and I are called to in Christ is not based on our ability but rather on His faithfulness. While our calling by God is sure because of His faithfulness, it is our daily walk by faith that helps to erase whatever doubts the enemy may attempt to plant in our mind. The doubts will come and go because we have a tendency to stumble throughout our walk. When we hold fast to God's calling to be sure, we find that nothing can make us fall. Living with certainty in our calling from God ought to equip us to walk by faith no matter what.

87

Called To Be Sure

As you pray about being called to be sure, ask God to help you be fully aware of His faithfulness throughout all generations. Pray that you would look to Him for a certainty that overcomes your doubts. Pray for an increased faith that gives you a confidence in God's ability to pick you up when you stumble. Pray that the people around you would see your unfailing confidence in God even when you have doubts in yourself. Pray that your faith would grow beyond the doubts of the world.

_____

_____

_____

_____

_____

_____

_____

_____

_____

_____

_____

_____

Day Twenty-Eight

Called

Through the Gospel

(2 Thessalonians 2:14)

Called Through the Gospel

How often do you read the Bible? Do you view it as just a book, or as words written to you? Why? How good is the news that the world publishes each day? Why? What would happen if you looked for, and shared, good news instead of the usual fare that gets talked about in most social circles? How does the good news of the Bible call you, and others, to a changed life? How does being called by God through the gospel influence the way you relate to God and the way you share that gospel with others?

In a world in which everything has been brought into existence by the word of God, the power of the gospel ought to be obvious. While some view the Bible as just a book, or a collection of old words, God says it is "the power of God which leads to salvation." Just as God called the elements of creation into existence by His Word, He calls each one of us to salvation through the good news of the gospel. Words are very powerful things and can be used to lift up or tear down. When we are confident of our calling through the gospel of Jesus, our words to others ought to be good news that shares that same gospel with them.

Called Through the Gospel

As you pray about being called through the gospel, ask God to help you trust Him as the true source of good news. Pray that you would hold fast to God's Word as the powerful force that it is. Pray that your time spent reading the Bible would encourage you as you allow its Author to speak His words to you. Pray that God's calling through His gospel would fill you with light in the midst of darkness. Pray that you would share the good news of Jesus with everyone you can.

_____

_____

_____

_____

_____

_____

_____

_____

_____

_____

_____

_____

_____

Day Twenty-Nine

Called

To Be Wanted

(Mark 3:13)

Called To Be Wanted

Have you ever been left out of something that you really wanted to belong to? How did you feel? Why? What does knowing you are wanted do for your attitude and sense of well-being? How about when you don't feel wanted? Which feeling do you have most often? Why? What things make you believe you are wanted? How can you help others to know they are wanted? Do you often think about Jesus calling you to Himself because you are wanted by Him? How does that make you feel? How do you share that with others?

When Jesus began His ministry on earth, He called to himself those He wanted. While some, such as the twelve disciples, are named, it becomes apparent throughout the gospels that He called many to Himself. In fact, He called, and continues to call, all who are thirsty to come and drink from the well that never runs dry. In the midst of your life, whether alone or in a crowd, Jesus calls you because He wants you to be with Him. Living as one called to be wanted by God ought to help you know your true value. As you join with all who are wanted by God, He equips you to help others know they too are wanted.

Called To Be Wanted

As you pray about being wanted by God, ask Him to fill you with confidence regarding His desire for you to be with Him. Pray about how God would have you encourage those who feel unwanted. Pray that being wanted by God would change not only the way you view yourself, but also the way you view others. Pray for a heart that is changed by an awareness of being wanted by God. Pray that your changed heart would help others to know they are wanted by God, and by you.

_____

_____

_____

_____

_____

_____

_____

_____

_____

_____

_____

_____

Day Thirty

Called

To Win the Prize

(Philippians 3: 14)

Called To Win the Prize

Have you ever won anything that you knew would never have been possible to obtain on your own? How does winning even small things make you feel? Why? How much does the encouragement of others help you to continue seeking something they believe you can obtain? Would you be more likely to enter a contest if the person in charge indicated you would win if you didn't give up? Why? In that light, how does being called by God to win the prize influence your desire to press on through whatever comes in life?

I used to get letters in the mail that were very clearly marked on the outside, "You may have already won!". While those were intriguing, the little word "may" often kept me from doing anything to win the potential prize. When God calls us to win the prize, there is no maybe involved — at least not in His willingness to give. It is our faithfulness in pursuing Him, not our perfection in doing so, that results in our receiving the prize for which we are called heavenward. Knowing that the prize of eternity with God awaits us, our goal each day ought to be to walk with Jesus in such a way that others see Him in us.

Called To Win the Prize

As you pray about being called to win the prize, ask God to fill you with the desire to be faithful. Pray that you would live with a confidence in God's ability to deliver the prize for which He has called you to receive. Pray that your relationship with God would help you to keep your eyes fixed on the eternal prize He offers. Pray that you would walk faithfully with God each day as you not only anticipate the prize that is to come, but as you share that prize with others.

Day Thirty - One

Called

To Be Worthy

(Ephesians 4: 1)

Called To Be Worthy

Are you worthy? How difficult is it for you to answer that question? Why? How is being worthy different from being counted worthy that was a devotion earlier in this book? Why? What/who determines if you are worthy? Explain. What makes people worthy to you — is it the way they feel or the way you feel about them? Explain. Since God has called you to be worthy, what does that say about how He feels about you? How can you help others know God calls them to be worthy? Will you?

While it is comforting to be counted worthy by God, it is perhaps more sobering to have God call me to be worthy. When I look deep within my life and know I am not worthy, there is hope in knowing that God looks even deeper and still calls me to be worthy. As one created in the image of God, He knows full well the potential that lies beneath the layers of crud I have accumulated in my life. When God calls me to live a life worthy of His calling, he makes it possible by transforming my heart and mind with the presence of His Spirit. When I live by the Spirit rather than by the flesh, I find I can be worthy of His calling.

Called To Be Worthy

As you pray about being called to be worthy, ask God to help you see His great love for you and the worth you have to Him. Pray that you would seek to live a life worthy of His calling as you allow His Spirit to make that possible. Pray for the courage to reject life choices that would not be worthy of God's presence. Pray that God's love would help you to see yourself as He sees you. Pray that your view of others would take place through the eyes of God as He deems them worthy of His love.

_____

_____

_____

_____

_____

_____

_____

_____

_____

_____

_____

_____

Bonus Day

Living

a Sacred Calling

(1 Corinthians 12:4-6

Colossians 3:23-24)

Living a Sacred Calling

What makes something sacred? How do you feel about your life being sacred? How does your consideration and practice of the things outlined in this devotional change the way you view a sacred calling? Why? Does the sacredness of your life's work come from what that work is or from who it is being done for? Explain. What things change, or should change, when you begin to view the everyday tasks of your life as part of your sacred calling from God? How will your view of others change when you acknowledge their work as a response to God's sacred calling in them?

When we live life set apart for God's use, everything is on the table. Responding to a sacred calling may involve preaching by some, but it is just as likely to involve welding by others. While we tend to define people by what they do occupationally, God is much more interested in who we are really doing it for. The previous thirty-one devotions in this book have all been written with the prayer that you will see your life, and your life's work, as a sacred calling from God regardless of how He has gifted you. As God calls, it is my prayer that each of us would respond, "Here am I".

Living a Sacred Calling

As you pray about living a sacred calling, thank God for giving you purpose in life. Pray that you would know the value of living a life set apart for God's exclusive use. Pray that you would make all of your gifts and abilities available for God to use as He sees fit. Pray for the humility needed to appropriately, and equally, value the sacred calling God has made to the people around you who have tasks which are different from yours. Pray that you would learn to help others pursue a sacred calling in the midst of everyday life.

_____

_____

_____

_____

_____

_____

_____

_____

_____

_____

_____

_____

Made in the USA
Middletown, DE
07 October 2022